Tarzan's Jungle Plane

Tarzan's Jungle Plane

prose poems

by Michael Malan

BLUE LIGHT PRESS ◆ 1ST WORLD PUBLISHING

BLUE LIGHT PRESS
1ST WORLD
PUBLISHING

SAN FRANCISCO ◆ FAIRFIELD ◆ DELHI

1ST WORLD LIBRARY
PO Box 2211
Fairfield, IA 52556
www.1stworldpublishing.com

BLUE LIGHT PRESS
www.bluelightpress.com
Email: bluelightpress@aol.com

COVER ART
Gabrielle Gern

AUTHOR PHOTOGRAPH
Roberta Sperling

FIRST EDITION

Library of Congress Control Number: 2019947274

ISBN 9781421836355

for my teachers

CONTENTS

III. A LIGHT WENT ON IN THE INVISIBLE TOWER

I. Torn Flowers and Reflected Highways

Three Great Treasures

I had a perfect childhood. My mom and dad and brother John were all best friends. John and I respected our parents and never got into trouble. Our grades were good and we were popular at school. We were never lonely, my brother and I, we did everything together. When I was in the fourth grade, we discovered the Hardy Boys and read all of the books in the series, some, like *The Disappearing Floor*, more than once. We had a dog, Harvey, who slept on our beds at night and ran bases with us when we played baseball. Each year, at Christmas, Santa brought us wonderful presents: a Lionel train, a Fort Apache play set, Tom Corbett's space station. Cereal boxes of sugary treats contained plastic animals. Movies downtown on Saturday afternoons were joyous fun. School was always a wonderful opportunity to learn more about astronomy, paleontology, literature, geography, and geometry. Every problem had a solution. We followed *The Three Musketeers* on their numerous adventures, reading each page aloud, each chapter as slowly as we could to make the book last forever. We were like Frank and Joe Hardy; every encounter, every experience was an adventure. "There are three great treasures," Mom told us. "A pure heart, the ability to love, and a Godly family. We are all living in the kingdom of heaven. Love is everywhere."

Early to Bed

From my upstairs room, I hear the lowing of cattle, the clinking of dishes in the kitchen, the soft voices of my parents in the living room. Joy opens all the doors of my house and the unrestricted play of every faculty. In her bedroom, my grandmother opens the trunk at the foot of her bed. She takes a drink of rye whiskey from the bottle she has hidden under the blankets. The red color in her cheeks is now restored. She comes into my room and kisses me goodnight. She moves freely from one room to the next, her good mood like a trumpet announcing her benevolent presence. Everywhere she goes there is movement. While I was at school, my mother rearranged our furniture. Yesterday, there were bunk beds in my room; tonight I have twin beds. When I fall asleep, I will float across the rivers and mountains to my birthplace in Montana. Eventually I will stop dreaming about the way things used to be—or the dream of who I was will become who I am.

Everything We Believe

And so I thought: what is solid, what is not? The Force nevers ebbs in the light-sabered forest. Nothing slipping away is still nothing. Smoke and shadows, trial and error. To be awake and aloof to improbabilities suggests a path of pine needles and cobwebs, the abstract reduced to something less than an unintended departure. A bicycle left standing in the rain, a waterfall bursting from the edge of a newly discovered world. Just before sleeping, an awareness of reaching out, trying to examine my own conscience, hoping to forget everything I learned in my youth. I can describe all the details with my eyes closed. At first, thoughts are melancholy, the bed in my room seems to take on a life of its own. A friend asks why the young die in car accidents. *Is it God?* No, I say, it's bad luck—or human error. Everything we believe is refined by circumstances we can't ignore. Today, we are entering a season of joy and celebration, shouts of praise, small rubber footballs tossed back and forth in the front yard.

My Mother's House

When my father died, the trees around our house vanished. When my mother died, the house moved away. *Don't make any changes for a year,* a friend advised, but the house moved to a cliff beside the ocean. I found the house years later when I was driving my red convertible on the shore road. A storm had come in from the sea and washed the house blue. The windows were closed, boarded up, and the front door was ajar. Should I take the house home and rebuild it, I wondered, or push it out to sea, let it be a boat and sail beyond the setting sun? When I think of my parents, I remember their thoughtfulness and patience. *Let the house be itself,* my father might say. *And let the ocean be the ocean.* I drove on, past memories of highways unfurling around monuments to the past, ancient cities, farmhouses, rustic cabins, and canvas tents. Lives redeemed in the pursuit of heavenly dreams. *Let the Spirit take you home,* my mother would say. *Be the house, be the ocean.*

Blast from the Past

Eric was reading a book when suddenly, unexpectedly, his TV turned itself on. Walter Cronkite was reporting the news. On the wall behind Walter was a map of Vietnam. He was talking about troop movements, a place called Hue, and a time of the year associated with heavy storms. A commercial break followed: the Frito Bandito had landed on Mars. Eric switched off the TV and looked around the room. The furniture had been re-arranged, but he couldn't remember when. "Good grief," he said and checked bigstory.com for the latest news. UFOs were landing in Washington, D.C. A creature from outer space was making demands that humans could never accept. Eric opened the window and looked outside. Helicopters were flying overhead, missiles striking a village, people fleeing. He closed the window and went back to reading *Where Did Our Love Go*, a book about the 1960s. Eric was born in 1984, so he doesn't remember any of it first-hand. He recalls that men landed on the moon in 1969 and that Martin Luther King freed African Americans from slavery about the same time. And Abe Lincoln was hunting vampires in Illinois—or maybe that came later. If you try hard enough, it's easy to smoke out the truth, Eric thought.

Beyond the Sea

I'd driven four hundred miles, jogged through swamp and death-is-life news reports, slow hours wrestling my fears to the edge of consciousness. Coffee at White Castle, thinking about Whitechapel and Jack, a failed surgeon, mutilating working girls who didn't know how to read or write or make change. The cashier holding my cup down until it stops thrashing. That far-and-wide look in her eyes. *Merrily, merrily, life is but a dream.* "The ocean is the ocean," she says, "a part of me. Do you know what I mean?" "I'm not sure," I say, wondering if she needs to take a break. It's late, almost midnight. "I'm sorry," she says. "My mother just died. She lay in bed for three months before she passed away. Friends came to visit. Relatives called. I sat at a card table and worked jigsaw puzzles—a castle in Bavaria, cover art for *Sgt. Pepper's Lonely Hearts Club Band*. There are so many things I don't understand. Why some die young and beautiful when they should live forever. Why time moves in a circle rather than a straight line. Why the sea is smooth like a carpet, then rough like an orange. Why a blush is like a dream or an island a planet within a circle. Why some are healed through prayer and others are still drifting. All these questions come back to me as I sail my silver ship across the ocean."

Blue Pills

I was feeling a little low, so I went to a Complete Nutrition store to get some vitamins. "I'm looking for something that will give me a boost," I said to Bob, who worked at the store. Bob reached into the pocket of his white smock and pulled out a bottle of blue pills. "Take one of these," he suggested. I grabbed the bottle, swallowed several pills. Minutes passed. Bob's appearance was changing rapidly, his long hair and smock a blur. He was spinning like a dervish. "Hey, what's going on?" I wondered. It was too late. Bob was gone, spun into another dimension. I looked around the store. On the wall was a painting of the Giza Pyramids at sunrise—a man on a blanket was praying at the edge of the desert. Hieroglyphics were scrawled in the sky. Esoteric symbols, fragments of text, twisted cuneiforms flowing through time. For a moment, I was in Egypt, riding a small Arabian horse. A gang of bedouins was following me on camels. I took another blue pill—*whoosh*—Bob reappeared. "Those are some pills," I said. Bob acted as though nothing unusual had happened. He slid something into a brown paper bag. "If you liked those blue pills," he said, "you'll like this." When I got home, I opened the bag. It was like looking up at the sky at night. A thousand stars twinkled. A distant sun burst into flames. I was back at the beginning, the dawn of time. A voice speaking in Arabic said: "Some say Mohammed disappeared in a flash of light. Others say they see him everywhere."

Hobart's Car

One summer I spent a few months on an Indian reservation. I'd heard Native Americans have a different time sense and some of them claim they can actually see corn growing. What I heard was true. The corn grew several inches while I was there. Great, big, golden ears. One of the women made corn bread and we sat around a campfire eating and telling stories. One of the men, Hobart, told how he had been hunting in the western part of the reservation and gotten lost in the hill country around Diablos Pequeños. "When I got back to my car, it was a mess," Hobart said. "The chassis had rusted out and the engine wouldn't start. I was sitting there wondering what to do, and a man came along and told me there had been a flash flood while I was gone. Some sort of angry spirit had come up out of the earth and ruined my car." Many of us found this hard to believe, but Hobart's friend, Carlos, vouched for his story. "It could be the beginning of something important. A glimpse of the future. Maybe we are entering into what my grandfather called the Fourth World." Lights flashed in the air around his head. I looked at my hands and saw the deep cuts of arroyos, corn blazing in the canyons of the sun, the earth reborn and swimming in space like the eye of the universe.

Broken Mirrors

Daniel and Natalie met at the New Ebenezer Baptist Church in Harlem and fell in love. They were blessed with two children and a dog. The children grew up and moved away, the dog died. Daniel grew restless and wanted to travel on his own. "I have a lot to think about," he told Natalie as he packed his bag for a long trip. In Barcelona, he fell in love with Martina, a woman he met at the Sagrada Familia. He learned to write poetry and play a guitar. Meanwhile, in New York, Natalie grew bitter and rented a studio apartment on the Upper West Side. Her lonely heart was a flickering torch, a shadow in the park, a bark in the night.

A few years later, Martina died in a car accident and Daniel moved back to the States. He and Lauren met at a rooftop bar in New York and fell in love, but it didn't last. Daniel was jealous and possessive, Lauren overly sensitive and immature. They drifted apart, spent years with people they didn't love, wandering from place to place, feeling that something was missing. Eventually, Lauren moved to Florida to live with her sister. Daniel bought a house in San Francisco that had been partially destroyed in an earthquake. He replaced the broken mirrors with a wall of trees, torn flowers and reflected highways, a dozen leaping oceans.

The Forever Universe

I had gone to a football game in Bayport and sat in a box seat overlooking the fifty-yard line. The smiles on the faces of the spectators were like beacons in the sky. One of the cheerleaders leaned forward; the sign of the crooked arrow had been tattooed on her breast. The air turned cold and voluptuous, small planets floated like mirrors in space. After the game, I drove home through a cloud of blue light. In a dream that night, I was walking on a busy street in an unfamiliar city. I passed a woman wearing a white dress. *The eternal elohim is the forever universe,* she said and smiled. The next morning I looked up "elohim" and found this: "the gods caused me to wander." I remembered Sunday school and how the ancient prophets could feel the presence of God when they were totally at one with the universe. I decided to shave my head and beard. I wish I could say I looked like Michael Jordan, but I looked more like Abraham or Lot, the bald one, just before God knocked the socks off Sodom and Gomorrah. The mirror disappeared and I was in Cairo surrounded by girls with dead eyes and filthy, screaming babies. I handed out ten-piaster notes to the most emaciated, too far gone to say *shukran.*

Just the Beginning

Sometimes the apparitions are religious, sometimes they are duplicitous, like I am not a ghost, but I am. I was in this bar, but not that one. I had one drink, maybe two. I drove home sober, woke up in a less-than-perfect world. My mother cooked my favorite breakfast, French toast, and we talked about how glorious the weather was. But then she suggested that maybe I should start looking for a job, stop playing Call of Duty so much, and try to meet some people my own age. Who needs that kind of pressure, I thought—if the way forward is just "do this, do that," I'd rather go back to school, watch violent history shows on HBO, or drive up and down the freeway, looking for adventure. And in that moment when the ghosts reappear, be someone else, a slice-and-dice Roman gladiator or prince so-and-so in boxer shorts. The Silver Surfer or Tony Stark lounging on the beach at St. Tropez. Black Panther or the Grinch that stole whatever. Someone like that. It's a glorious day.

The Cabin in the Forest

Two men are sitting in front of a cast-iron stove. As I untie my moccasins I think about the trap I set on the trail that leads to a frozen stream. I have so many vivid memories: the Upper West Side in New York City, where I thought only of myself and felt no fear of death. The Gold Country in California, where I found a human skull on the banks of the American River. Egypt, where I cut open a tangerine and it was full of maggots. Pine Ridge, where death followed me every night on the Trail of Wandering Spirits. I thought there might be some answers there, along the river that flowed beside the Sacred Mountains, but there wasn't, nothing made sense. And now, as I warm my hands before the wood stove, someone sighs deeply—there are more than two men here. I will find out who they are and what they want. First, though, I will search for the map my ancestors left in a trunk in the attic. I go upstairs. Birds swirl in the rafters, squirrels have eaten a hole in the roof. The trunk is empty. I see the midnight sky, but no stars.

Festival

B.B. King is performing at Ravinia, an outdoor music festival north of Chicago. Jean-Paul, who is 25-years-old, is having trouble focussing, even though the music embraces the power of the wind and fields and forests that stretch toward Canada, crossing a multitude of lakes where lean young men are swimming and boating. Alain, the oldest in their group, is speaking French to a woman who is sitting beside him. She gestures as though she understands most of what he says. Something about a *bateau* or *fleuve* and how Alain felt when he arrived in Paramaribo on a day when it was almost too hot to breathe. "The thrill is gone," B.B. King is singing in his deep river voice. Alain is sitting on a Pendleton blanket, leaning back on his hands, watching the performers and quoting Rimbaud: *"Il y a une cathédrale qui descend et un lac qui monte."* And the city behind them is sinking like a cathedral and the music is rising like a tidal wave. And Jean-Paul is channeling Rimbaud, who is walking on water with all the naked boys.

Heaven on Earth

I was sitting in my room thinking about the nature of reality, whether it is human or divine, whether there are individual souls or one big Spirit, and I got a glimpse of paradise that was pretty much the same as what the Jodie Foster character experienced in the movie *Contact*. My dad and I were standing on a long, crescent-shaped beach, and we were talking about cars and how sad we felt when we heard Dale Earnhardt had died in a fiery crash. A boat motored past and Dale Earnhardt was waterskiing from the back of the boat. My dad looked at me and we started laughing—just like that time, years ago, when we were driving home from a stock car race in Pocatello, Idaho, and he was telling me how he had never been outside the county where he grew up, until he was 18 and enlisted in the navy. Sent to Japan, his ship entered Tokyo Bay during the night, a heavy mist cloaking the city. The next morning, he and some other sailors were sent ashore and the fog lifted—Tokyo was the first city my dad had seen. When he finished the story, he started laughing, and I did, too. We had to pull the car over to the side of the road and wait until the laughing stopped. That was heaven. Heaven on earth.

Night Songs

Before I awake, a slow waking, I am a child in a farm-house, cows mooing outside. Then I am an old man, a saint living in a monastery, the floor is made of stone, and my feet are cold. And then I'm a teenager, late for break-fast and my father scolds me because I spend too much time in the bathroom getting my hair right. On the monastery wall is a poster, a crowd of people, and the words, "He taught them many things." The bed is small and the room cozy. Through the window I see the sun ris-ing. A bell is chiming. I will meet my brothers for lunch, take long walks in the evenings. A bird will perch on my shoulder, moonlight wrap itself around my legs. Night songs will rise like stars in an orchard of honey-colored apples. And when I'm fully awake I'll be standing on a subway platform—or is it a station for an elevated train? A bus whizzes past. I am late for work, a clerk in a ware-house in London, a salesman in a department store in Chicago. My friends come to see me off, stand around my bed, admire my poster. One says to the others: "He had compassion on them all."

Chippewa Street

Jonathon and Nicole met at a poetry reading. He suggested they have a drink, so they went to a bar on Chippewa Street. Jonathon thought the name of the street was cool and had always wanted to go there for a drink. Nicole felt that Chippewa Street would have some special meaning for her and that Jonathon might be a person with unusual gifts, that he might share some clever insight, a nugget of esoteric information, something that would change her life. They drank two bourbons and Jonathon went to the men's room. When he got back, Nicole was gone. "Hey," he said to the bartender, "do you know what happened to the woman who was sitting here?" The bartender was wiping the bar with a towel, his arms covered with tattoos. Jonathon noticed a rope-and-anchor tattoo on one forearm and the Hand of Fatima on the other. "I think she went upstairs with that pimp who was sitting at the end of the bar," the bartender said. Jonathon remembered the pimp's phosphorescent green suit, red felt hat, and high-top black shoes. He was very tall and thin and glanced back and forth like a weasel. "Oh shit," Jonathon said and collapsed on a stool. "Just kidding," the bartender said. "Have a drink on me." He pushed a shot glass across the bar and topped it off with crème de menthe. "Her mother called and she went to the hospital. Her dad had a stroke. She'll call as soon as she can."

The Poet and His Muse

Ashley is sitting by himself in an almost-empty room, just one chair, table, ashtray, box of cigars, overdue library book, *The Doors of Perception*. "When I was nineteen," he writes in a notebook, "I was imprisoned in a novel written by a woman whose prospects for marriage were nil. Things are different now. People don't like power relationships." He is depressed by what he has written and sits for a long time looking out the window. Miss Scarlett enters the room and hands him a photograph. He studies the photo for several minutes. "Is this your father?" he asks her. "It is, mister." He raises his eyebrows, puffs pensively on his Swisher Sweet. "You sound more like Mammy than Scarlett," he says. "I'm sorry, mister," she says, not looking him in the eye. He gets up, stands staring down at her lovely frying-pan coiffure. "Do you remember the Grateful Dead?" he asks. "Of course I do," she says, and hums a few bars of "Uncle John's Band." He sits down and begins writing furiously, filling pages of a yellow legal pad with poetic scribblings. The sun sets. He looks up. There is no bed in this room, he realizes. Where will I sleep?

A Man of Means

All Alice wanted was a man with money. Her first beau, Gerald, was good-looking, but had no prospects. She left him for Diamond Jim, who, in spite of his name, was penniless. They broke up after two years of living in flop houses, abandoned cars, and homeless shelters. In the fall of 2010, she met Cedric, a banker, but he had a great many debts and the relationship ended badly. A few months after they broke up, he wrecked his yacht in a windstorm off the coast of Nantucket. And then there was Tobias, who had been born rich, but after years of living in luxury hotels, gave all his money to the Salvation Army and wandered from city to city like a hobo, sleeping in the entryways of department stores and church porticos. Her most recent lover, Rupert, is the most impoverished of them all. He lost everything hunting for rubies in the Punjab district of India and now camps on a dunghill south of Mysore. Bitten by a cobra, he lost touch with reality and spends his days reciting passages from Kipling's least-revered novels. He is especially fond of *Gunga Din*. As they sit together on a ragged camel hide, Alice is beginning to think her dream of finding a man with money will never be realized. "Honey," she says, "are you going to sit here all your life? I feel like I'm stuck, energy draining through my feet into sacred space." "I know what you mean," Rupert says. "I feel the same way. Let's find an abandoned car or mud hut where we can think things through more carefully." "I'm tired of thinking," she says. "Let's go home, get jobs, live like regular people." "Whatever you say," Rupert says, although secretly he is not very optimistic. Even lottery winners get the blues.

Something Large

During the last days of the Great Recession, I spent a lot of time in airports listening to conversations and jotting down bits of dialogue. It's not easy to explain, but it was at O'Hare, waiting for a flight to Atlanta, that I found my voice. A line from a John Ashbery poem kept drifting through my head: "Everything has a schedule, if you can find out what it is." And then, for just a few minutes, I was someone else, an Old Testament minor prophet, stranded in Manitoba like a prairie populist. I stood on street corners in Medicine Hat and recited poetry—Emily Dickinson mostly, or Sir Walter Scott: "The stag at eve had drunk his fill, where danced the moon on Monan's Rill." Most of the conversations I had with passers-by were short and sweet, like Canadian summers. In my prayer meeting last night I tried to talk about the unity of being, but my evangelical friends would have none of it. In olden days, it was considered unwise to fall asleep in the bath or hunt elk under a harvest moon. Today we are more attuned to the primal scream. Something large is looming on the horizon.

Writing Workshop

I'd been revising an old poem, reconstructing, deconstructing—trying to resuscitate the stillborn. But when I took it to class, the teacher said, "Oh no, you've made it worse. Shine a little light in the dark places." More revisions and I was stuck with a conception I didn't want: like in *Eraserhead,* the thing was wrapped in burlap, and it screamed all night long. "Throw in some pizzle and snoop," the teacher said next time we met, "verbs that huff and puff and don't just lie there and vegetate." At home, I got my compressor out of the garage and pumped up the poem like a basketball. The next morning, it had gone flat again. "Add an invoice, a memo, or a shopping list," the teacher ranted, so I dug up a short note from a former lover and inserted it here: *Michael, don't ever call or write again.* "Not bad," the teacher said. "At least you've got the balls to share your pain. But it could be better. Get some power tools and really go after it, like in *The Texas Chain Saw Massacre* or one of those slasher movies." But I'm not sure I have enough repressed rage or hostility or whatever it takes, so I locked the poem in the basement for a week, until it got real hungry, then I turned it loose at the student union. A few days later, another email: *I'm sorry. I didn't mean it. Please call. I miss you.*

Tarzan's Jungle Plane

Most legends originate elsewhere, in the middle of a busy street or across a wavy ocean, in another curriculum. The natives get down and done when the sun sets and the city fathers and mothers are too busy to apologize for the unity of being. It's not the suburban blueprint most people desire—we prefer to shake our booties until the sun rises, throw open the door, invite everyone in. Share some pink grapefruit and double whammies, jungle juice, barbecued carabao. A glimpse of my sister's fabulous kneecaps. She's precocious, you bet, but not above the Temptations. *Sweet soul music.* It's like the sky's on fire, one apeman after another, a log-jam of crocodiles in a raging river. It's never too late to come down from your tree, move to a swamp, or parade back and forth in front of imaginary mirrors. Stay out all night on the veldt, let the monkey fly the plane. He and Jane separated, but still friends. "Don't stop," Tarzan says. "Fly straight on."

Museum Opening

We are standing around a grand piano. Men wearing black formal clothes, women floor-length dresses. I'm wearing a pale blue jacket and Mondrian tie. My shoes have not been polished since Bill Clinton was president. Alexander Bertalovski, the 19th-century curator, is standing next to my wife, Carol, his new assistant, glass of champagne in his hand, looking at me and smiling. "And what do you do?" he asks. "I'm unemployed," I say proudly, like I retired early. Except I'm only 32, we just moved here from California, and I don't have a job. The piano stops. I hear spiders crawling on the wall. The paintings shiver. My Mondrian tie chokes me. My brown shoes walk away and leave me barefoot, choked. Cameras flash. I'm on nationwide television. All eyes on me. Loud thoughts: *He seems whole. He has both arms and legs. Could he be retarded?* I look at Carol. Smile frozen on her face. "He's a writer," she says brightly, and they nod solemnly, like that explains everything. Clever boy. Clever girl.

Five Postcards

Our relationship was hot and cold over several years, off and on, breaking up, then getting back together, heaven and hell. I was watching *X-Men United* thinking about Agent Smith fighting with Laurence Fishburne on top of a speeding truck in *Matrix Reloaded*. Or was it Snake Plissken getting stabbed in the leg just as he was about to rescue the president in *Escape from New York?* I guess I wasn't really listening when Katelyn told me she was leaving for good. I had been faithful for the most part (no penetration, just some hot kissing and fondling), so I was shocked when she told me she had slept with two of my best friends. I love truth, honesty, being open with one another, but there are times when things are best left unsaid. Her first postcard was from Killdeer, North Dakota: "Still haven't found what I'm looking for. Will write soon." When I received her second postcard from the Mojave Desert, I could almost smell the desert sage and manzanita trees. People ask me where she is, why she didn't move to Barcelona and marry the young Spaniard who proposed to her while they were standing at the base of Multnomah Falls. "I almost jumped overboard," she wrote from Skagway. Her last postcard was from Guatemala: "Volcán de Fuego erupted today and destroyed the *pensión* where I was staying. Now every Sierra Madre knows my name."

World Traveler

"We have so much," Marsha told her friends. "We can fly everywhere. France, Japan, you name it." She flew to Timbuktu just to prove she could do it. On her way back, the plane was hijacked and landed on a mysterious island off the coast of Burma. The passengers were swept aside. "We just want the plane," one of the hijackers said. After the plane took off, Marsha sat on the beach with the other passengers around a driftwood fire. "Why did they want that plane?" someone asked. "It's all we had," Marsha said. "They could have taken our bodies," one of the women said. The men laughed. "What's so funny?" Marsha asked. The men looked at each other, or at the ocean, which was rising, getting higher, just like the environmentalists predicted. A week later, they were rescued. The airline offered them free flights to anywhere they wanted to go. "It's the least we can do," the airline agent said. Marsha wanted some place dangerous. It's in her blood now. Dense jungles, empty deserts, frozen wastelands. The sky is an ocean of wind and clouds. The moon is a lamp in the pilot's hand.

Bliss

After she graduated from Cornell, Susan married a man who was immature, intemperate, and promiscuous. Susan believed he would change. He would learn to love her and become a model citizen, a considerate husband and father. Instead, he started drinking heavily and using recreational drugs. Eventually, she divorced him and started dating Seth, who belonged to an evangelical church. He refused to have sex before they were married. He believed they should develop a "spiritual friendship" from which an "emotional connection" would follow. "Physical intimacy" would come later, after they were married and could afford to have children. Susan worried that Seth would find her unattractive when they were naked together. Could she satisfy him sexually—or "physically," as he described it? One night she dreamed that his penis was overly large and she woke up in a fright. As it turned out, they lived happily ever after. Seth was a wonderful companion and they had two beautiful children. They were married for fifty years and then Seth died, or "passed on," as he would say. Susan joined a church group of women who had "lost" their husbands. Their relations were warm and satisfying. They shared pictures and stories of their grandchildren. When Susan passed on, she and Seth were reunited in heaven where they exist in the realm of eternal bliss. Love conquers all.

II. Time Was Like a Curtain Inside a Mirror

In the Heart of the City

Allison was born and raised in the country, but moved to the city to look for a job. She meets Travis, who was born and raised in the city. When he looks in her eyes, he sees cornfields, endless pastureland, windmills, and railroad crossings. When she looks in his eyes, she sees back alleys, skyscrapers, and anonymous high-rise apartment buildings. He sees family picnics, church socials, covered wagons crossing the Great Plains. She sees gangsters, bootleggers, hucksters, and deal-makers. He wants to be rich, he tells her, and buy a new car every two years. She will never be rich, she knows, and neither will he, because wealth is inherited, never earned, and the man from the city was born into poverty. He will live his life as a laborer, drink stale beer and eat red meat. He will never compromise his masculinity. She wants to be happy, she tells him, raise healthy children and grandchildren, sit on her porch Sunday evenings and wave to neighbors as they walk home from potluck dinners and bingo parties at the Elks Club. He looks in her eyes and sees dust storms and tornadoes. She sees earthquakes, power outages, and crime sprees. They nod knowingly at each other, pick up their lunch trays, and go back to work. Desire seeps from her skin to become the fields that nourish her.

Twins

One summer, when we were in college, my twin sister and I shared a job at the Belle Vue Motel in the Adirondacks. She worked one day, I worked the next. We made beds, cleaned toilets, vacuumed up after messy lovers and loners munching their way through long nights in the middle of nowhere. At the end of August we went into the office to pick up our last check. Marvin, the manager, looked at us and blinked, then tried to refocus. This is my sister, I told him, and Misty smiled. "You don't look at all alike," he said, even though, every morning, every other day, one of us had dropped by his office to pick up the master key, and he tried, rather lamely, to be charming and friendly. "I guess not," I said and looked at Misty and laughed. "Didn't he ask you out?" "No, it must have been you," she said. Marvin laughed. "Very funny," he said. "See you next summer." "Maybe you could hire both of us," Misty said. "Sure. Whatever. I've got a brother. We could double date." The idea of two Marvins was too much—this one looked like a boxer who had lost most of his fights—and we did not return to the Belle Vue Motel. After graduation, Misty and I moved to Twinsburg, Ohio. We still have the same thoughts, the same feelings, the same memories. We are never alone. Never.

Whatever Comes Our Way

The day I met Sonya she was lying on a dark green blanket reading *The Golden Notebook*. Her hair was bushy, wild, and her smile seductive. I told her I only wanted to work part-time and she told me she felt the same way: *Let's live life on the road. Take me somewhere I have never been before.* We drove across America in my battered Subaru, blue highways mostly, sleeping in state parks and seedy motels. We spent hours wading in creeks, swimming in mountain rivers, shagging the waterfalls for healing spirits. Amusement of light and water, sky buried in ancient flame, earth and air tangled in deep space. We crawled out of our tent at midnight, stars falling in the Big Dipper, miniature galaxies hovering in the buffalo grass. In the Dakota Badlands, the trail was mostly uphill in the hot sun across a barren Dead Sea terrain. Bible passages kept coming at me, slipping past the first level of consciousness and going straight to the Truth. We are not animals, but plants that can't stop moving. We must be careful about Money.

Excerpts from *The Book of Hosanna*

You are walking on a narrow path through jagged mountains. Green birds are nesting in lemon-colored trees. For the first time, you see life as it really is, how it was meant to be. *When the eyes of the ox are covered, he will turn the mill wheel. When his eyes are uncovered, even the snow cannot see him.*

•

In the wilderness each leaf is a tiny planet. The path through the mountains is lit by a purple sunset. You have given up all thought of good and evil. *In the presence of the Redeemer, you must answer for your whole life. Only then will you understand the wind as it becomes unraveled.*

•

When Jesus ascended into Heaven, he healed a blind man, who was also lame and epileptic. "Go, and sin no more," the Lord said. "Your faith has made you whole." *Avoid those who argue. Their dreams have solidified, and their hands are hopelessly waving in the air.*

•

You are walking on a path between low hills and poppy-covered fields. In the sky are planets drawing blood from the earth. You are feeling at one with God, but your toe hurts. *Just as fish die on dry land, so monks must dwell apart from the ghost of laborious.*

•

Grim deities stand in the field like statues. You have lost, not just one, but several of your favorite sheep. You are a shadow, as transparent as the air around a mountain peak. *Overcome the temptation to wink at life. Otherwise the gray beard of winter will absorb your fingerprint*

•

After a long journey, you arrive at a village where you are greeted by worldly Buddhas, the sons and daughters of temptation, one pure light. God moves every atom, every wave of thought. *When you have put into practice the ways of Heaven, solitude will uncork the trees of your heart.*

Only the Brave

My first trip into space was a rough ride with H. G. Wells in the back seat and Jules Verne riding shotgun. When we got to the moon, Verne said, "Let's keep going; I've always wanted to see Jupiter." We got lost for a light year in the rings of Saturn, and Wells told us a long story about invaders from Mars. That night I looked in my logbook and filled in the dots where Jupiter should be. Verne told us how he'd received the baptism of the Holy Spirit at a full gospel meeting in Bombay. "The mind moves from limitation to perfect freedom," Wells said. "The trajectory is an arc around the entire galaxy. When Artemis was a hunter, she lit a fire, and Orion, who had been her lover for many eons, disappeared—he eventually found his place among the stars. War ceased and the harmony of all mankind was guaranteed. Only the brave can find the planet that is reborn every night in the soul of restless peace." We thought about that for a while, maybe a century in Earth terms, and then there was the long trip home, through vistas of intense flashing lights, exploding suns, and shattered rainbows. When we got back to Earth, everyone we knew had died, but we were immune to change. Now we sit with those who wait and take notes when the voices speak.

Star of A.

Josh got some Attitude. A six-ounce bottle for $17.95, a bargain. He won't drink it all at once, just when he needs it. A little sip before breakfast maybe, when his dad says hi. He'll take a jolt at lunch in the school cafeteria or on Sunday morning riding in the car to church, or when his mom asks him to do something, or he has to write a report, or answer a question in class. "Who was the leader of the British government during World War II?" the teacher asks. "Winston. Churchill," Josh says. "Churchill" dripping with A. "And he was?" "Prime. Minister." A. oozing from "prime," "minister" sizzling on a bed of red-hot A. coals. "Very good," the teacher says, and smiles. The other kids smile, too. Josh is the star of A. today. "Bravo," his friend Hector says as they walk down the hall, no longer boys, but men of A. They see one of the cheerleaders, Brittany Pearson, walking toward them. She looks at Josh for the first time and smiles, her eyes glowing like blue beacons. A. pays big dividends—the look in her eyes lights up every horizon he can imagine, every dark corner of the globe.

Positively

I'm reading a book about cats and how they fit in to the neighborhood. Cats wandering the streets on Halloween, black with ghostly concerns. I would like to hear their concerns, but most of the cats speak Danish, and Danish is a language I don't care to learn, so I avoid taking the courses. Not just the language courses, but all of the courses where I have to pay attention. My mind drifts and fantasies take the place of whatever people are saying. I see rocket ships and flying saucers in the eyes of the other students and the love of God in *Les Fleurs du Mal*. I think about Mary Shelley and Dr. Frankenstein and how most of us seem stapled together. I think about Shelley reading Poe, and Poe reading Hawthorne, and Hawthorne climbing inside a toy Bible with Ichabod Crane. Does that sound strange? I'll explain it all later, after the green light in the forest fades, and the blue light in my lampshade comes on like a star. And after school, when I'm feeling good again, as if I'm beginning to understand the mysteries of folklore, the gathering army of black cats, and the way some books seem to take on a life of their own—when all that happens, a cloud will descend and take my breath away. But I'll still be the same person, so glad to see you.

Everything's OK

Jake and I were sitting in his living room. Through the picture window I could see a snow-covered mountain on the other side of a blue-green valley and a waterfall splashing into the valley. "Have you read *A Confederate General from Big Sur*?" Jake asked me. I nodded. "Do you remember that the main characters never have any money? They shake down two kids for $6.72 and that's an enormous deal. They can't decide whether to buy food or bullets to hunt squirrels. That was back before the SNAP program. You know, food stamps." "Yeah, things are better now," I said, although listening to myself I didn't sound convincing. Just then, a man wearing a red-and-black checkered cowboy hat came out of one of the bedrooms. "I'm going into town," he said. "Do you want anything?" "No, I'm OK," Jake said. "So everything's Jake," the man in the cowboy hat said. "Yeah, I guess so," Jake said and they laughed. "That's my dad," Jake said, after the cowboy left. "He's more California than Colorado." I went outside. The sun was setting and the mountain and waterfall gradually disappeared. I went back inside. Jake was watching a *Star Wars* movie. R2D2 was beeping like a pinball machine. Jake was laughing. He was always laughing.

Shoplifters

Diego bought a pack of cigars and while the cashier was ringing it up I stole a small flashlight and a tin of Cherry Blend tobacco. We loved Swisher Sweets and Mag-Lites. Smoking cigars and corncob pipes made us feel like men. We sneaked out at night, roamed the black arteries of our small town, stole cantaloupes and watermelons. Flash-lights came in handy. In a backyard garden we found a marijuana plant and yanked it like a turnip. We smoked the buds and leaves and most of the stems until our brains turned to cigarette paper. Diego borrowed his brother's I.D. and we bought a case of Grain Belt beer, sailed his dad's boat up Big Stone Lake and camped in a secluded cove. We guzzled the beer, fell in the water fully clothed, laughing and pointing fingers at each other. Everything was funny. Until our stomachs rebelled and a bomb went off in my esophagus. Athena's lake temple turned purple and the flat beer capsized. It was not all bad. The transformation of two dumb tents is a blessing for every *Feliz Navidad*.

Summer of Love

Mr. Rock rarely gets stoned, except occasionally, after he watches TV for long time and his brain is numb. Then he goes down to the basement and digs out his secret stash. He fires up his hubbly-bubbly, smokes some fragrant marijuana, sits quietly in the dark and thinks about back in the day when he was a panhandler in San Francisco during the Summer of Love. "There wasn't really so much love then," Mr. Rock says to himself. "It was mostly flowers and drugs and fornication. But hey, that seemed like love." After the Summer of Love, Rock went to work on a ranch in Wyoming. It wasn't a hard job. Mostly he just did guard duty so that no one would steal the rancher's cattle. There were a lot of poachers in Wyoming after the Summer of Love. Rock worked on the ranch for nearly eight years until he fell off a bull at the Calgary Stampede and broke his leg in several places. The doctor told him it was the worst fracture he had ever seen. Unable to return to his job at the ranch, Rock went on disability and moved to Denver, where he lives now on Skid Row. He misses the ranch, the wide-open spaces, the mountains in the distance. "Those were good times," Mr. Rock thinks as he drops his marijuana pipe in a drawer and goes upstairs to get a glass of bourbon.

Off the Coast

I open the door and there he is. *Oh, it's you*, he says. I
try to remember when Ishmael first came to live with
me. It was after my wife left. He listened to my prob-
lems and never talked about himself. He spent most of
his time watching sports on television, knew the
names of most of the players, and kept his baseball
cards in a shoe box under the bed in my guest room.
But something changed. Now he tells me stories about
sailors on a ship off the coast of Skull Island. They
stand on the deck on warm sunny days and let the sun
soak in their pores. Rare birds nest in their hair. The
sea is calm, but the captain is uncomfortable. He won-
ders if mutiny might be close at hand. Days pass like
moonlight through a window, spiderwebs in his wash
basin. He dreams of sword-bearing skeletons, a
cyclops with cauliflower ears. He hears men whisper-
ing in unfamiliar languages. *Are they citizens of another
country? Travelers in a new kind of nexus?* When the sun
sets, the sailors scurry like insects below deck. The
captain reaches for a bottle of port. The first mate
appears, holding a beach ball. His beard has grown
longer and heavier overnight, reaching almost to his
waist. The ocean represents eternity, the captain
thinks, as his fear grows. An enormous white whale
surfaces off the starboard bow.

A Dangerous Woman

I was driving down Sunset Boulevard and Erika waved from her front porch. I parked my car and followed her inside. She handed me a piña colada with too much rum. It had been months since we'd seen each other. She'd been living in the Caribbean, teaching English at a detention center. While she was talking, I got a whiff of something dangerous, not that she could hurt me, but that I might grow up too soon and have to get a job, or I might stumble into something illegal and get caught. She turned her blue eyes on me like a searchlight. The warmth of the sun vanished. There was a nightmare chill in everything she said. I was Snow White and she was the Bride of Satan. Over her shoulder and slightly to her right, I saw a specter hovering, waiting to pounce. I left Erika's house and drove home, everything eerie, even on familiar streets. Green puddles had appeared on the pavement and the sodium-arc street lights at every intersection were far too bright. I saw her a few days later in the parking lot at Publix. Sitting there in my car, I had a vision of heaven: she and I were children again, growing up in happy homes. All the drugs and alcohol and sinful behavior disappeared as the planets realigned and cosmic sparks flew from one sun to the next. The earth melted and branches from the Tree of Life filled all space.

Genesis

God said to Adam, "Do some work, man. Make yourself useful." "I'm depressed," Adam said, "because I don't have a companion." "What?" God said. "You've got all these nice animals to play with. Brother Bear and Brother Fox—they're your friends." "There's something missing," Adam said. "Fox and Bear are too fuzzy. I want somebody smooth." "OK," God said, and created Eve to be Adam's companion. "Oh, good," Adam said. "Now someone else can work in the garden while I lie under the Tree of Life and daydream." At first, Eve was happy, but eventually she grew weary of toiling for her husband. It was cool in the garden, but planting tomatoes was hard work. Her ribs ached and her old man was a bore, always asking for more than he gave. She wanted a career in high finance, a nanny from Mexico, vacations in Paris and Rome. Eve knew exactly what she was doing. "Enough of this patriarchal bullshit," she said, and handed the magic apple to Adam.

Headshrinker

Jacoby went to a therapist to have his head examined. "Jacoby," the doctor said, "you need to get out more, meet some people, take a walk on the wild side." The next Friday night, Jacoby went to a singles bar, but everyone was sitting alone at their own tables and staring into the gloom. So he went to a doubles bar, but he was the only single there. "Do you know where I can find a triples bar?" he asked the bartender. The bartender looked at him like he had two heads. "My doctor says I should take a walk on the wild side," Jacoby said, so the bartender sent him to the wrong side of town where he was beaten and robbed. "It was awesome," Jacoby said when he saw his therapist the next week. "Those people know how to live." "Let's go down there," the doctor said. "I'd like to see some of that action first-hand." That night they took a bus to the wrong side of town. All the streetlights had been shot out. Windows everywhere were blank. It was like walking in a dark room, except they could see the vague shapes of buildings lit by the city behind them. "It's great, isn't it," Jacoby said, "like a black gauzy curtain over everything." Suddenly they were surrounded by swift, powerful young men who punched them several times and took their wallets. Jacoby and the doctor picked themselves up—everything was topsy-turvy—and staggered back to the bus stop. "Wasn't that great?" Jacoby said. "You bet," the doctor said. "I'm going to waive your fee."

Pathfinders

Driving through a forest, I hit a deer, then ran over a buffalo and flattened a mountain lion in my Humvee. "I'm glad we have a big car," my wife said. A coyote appeared, paws on its hips, doing a little dance at the side of the road. "Can you hit him?" she asked. The coyote was too quick and we smashed into a tree. "Timber!" I shouted as the tree hit the ground. "Let's make our own road through the forest," my wife said and we drove straight on, like a tank, giant firs snapping like twigs. At the ocean, I looked at her and she nodded. "Let's see if this baby floats." It didn't, of course, and we traveled many miles underwater until we found an off-ramp to the mainland. NORTH AMERICA 22 MILES, the sign said. That night, snug in our sleeping bags, we watched falling stars bounce off the hood of the car.

Changing My Life

I'd been watching *Something Wild,* the scene where Melanie Griffith and Jeff Daniels are dancing cheek-to-cheek at Melanie's high school reunion, an amateur band is playing "Fame," and Ray Liotta rises up from the floor like a specter. At that moment I resolved to change my life, jumped out the window, drove to Winn-Dixie and bought a dozen powdered donuts. I knew I needed to make some decisions, look for a job, get my fortune told, or start a business. Go back to school, get married, or buy a gun. This is the land of opportunity, I thought as I finished the last donut. I drove across town to visit Jason, a guy I met at the employment office. He was lying on a mattress, flies buzzing around his head. I told him about *Something Wild* and how Melanie was pretending to be someone else— Lulu, not Audrey, which was her "real" name in the film. Jason had a North Country passion for Melanie Griffith; his eyes were emoting blue rays that lit up all the walls in his dumpy apartment. His holy vision was like a peaceful morning in a high school classroom, the teacher reading *Pride and Prejudice,* and all the students suddenly awake to the nature of perfect being.

The East Window

Tired this morning, thinking about Byron the day after he heard Beethoven's sixth symphony and wandered into a field of poppies similar to the field next to the stream that flowed through Shelley's blue mountain dell, which was also "the resting place" of John Clare, who considered "The Triumph of Life" to contain some of Shelley's best work. He (Byron) wanted to blame the church for his misreading of the poem. There are papal spies everywhere, even in the 6th arrondissement, he believed. Not every statue in the Jardin du Luxembourg tells a story or even hints at what, in reality, the dispossessed feel at the beginning of each new day. A phrase in Latin popped into his head: *Nos patriae fines et dulcia linquimus arva.* Could it be the Venus flower had some relationship to the myth of Sisyphus? he wondered. Or was this just a matter of another night with the wrong woman? There are several versions of this story, not just one, I realized. Did Childe Harold sleep with a red-headed woman in Montmartre, or did he sleep on the floor next to her bed? Meanwhile, at Dove Cottage, the fever had passed and Wordsworth drew himself up into a figure from Homer. The body is not all substance and heat, he affirmed. Give God the glory. The east window in his study had become a door. He walked outside, through a field of poppies, his face a mirror of the past, his mind like a photograph of a sacred rose.

Just Yesterday

Last time I saw Uncle Jeff he was riding a silver wheel-chair in alcoholic heaven. Then he was lying on a beach in Maui, a big wave coming in, sand and water breaking down into green and purple dots, like a badly printed comic book. Gung-ho marines shouting and shooting their M-16s, Vietnamese women and children running naked through the streets of nameless American cities. I think I saw Jeff one more time as I was crossing the Golden Gate Bridge on a bus and he was plunging like a dummy into the bay. It might have been someone else though, a guy I knew in Ithaca, New York, who jumped from a suspension bridge into Cascadilla Gorge. Just yesterday I was lying on a blanket in Central Park listening to Lou Reed sing "Hey, babe, take a walk on the wild side," and a big shadow blacked out the sun. I went home and sat on the couch and thought about Aunt Dorothy, who drank too much and was hit by a bus. There was a poster on the door of three men like statues, perfectly cast as soldiers, bearers of good tidings, and a zero squeezed between the necks of marble birds. The room vanished and time was like a curtain inside a mirror, opening and closing, patterns of light on the wall, images from magazines with stark, anonymous covers. I lie awake every night, seeing the same star.

Under the Sign of Virgo

I told my mother I was in Bremerton, but I wasn't in Bre-
merton, I was in Bellingham visiting my ex, and I didn't
want my mother to know where I was, so I lied and told
her I was in Bremerton and went to a movie with some
friends. I told her the sky was black and a rainbow was
striding across Puget Sound. A little color helps make the
lies sound more real. I don't want to talk about last dates,
good-bye forever, that moment when you know it's over,
the door slams, a car pulls away and you're in Bremerton,
where you've never been, and there's a dent in the hood
of your car. A big dent. And then you are in Grants Pass
and the water in the Rogue River is exploding like the
heart of a small boy who is running beside a lake in Min-
nesota. And after sundown the sky above Shadow Moun-
tain is like a blue eye in the parking lot where you are
waiting for a biker to finish his ablutions in the men's
room, and you are thinking about how, after things settle
down, you will stop wandering and find a place to live in
Miles City or Belle Fourche and spend your evenings in
the backyard in a lawn chair so deep you will be like a fish
in the Sea of Light, and you won't forget to leave the win-
dow open so you can breathe.

The Art of Blessing

The second time I was arrested I was just standing on the corner, you know, not doing anything. Thinking about how the light on the buildings changes in the evenings and the houses look like facades in an Edward Hopper painting. The street was quiet, all the lawns had been rolled up and stowed away in backyard storage units. I was thinking about Lydia and how I had forgotten to call her when I got out of jail. I wasn't seeing very well—the cops had busted my glasses the first time they arrested me. They were talking about synapses and concussions and messages that had been read "by the pale moonlight." A car alarm went off and a dog howled. I held my breath waiting for the worst to happen. I don't mind being arrested, except all the knife fights in the prison cafeteria make me uncomfortable. I tell the men about Jesus and they, most of them, want to hear more. Their thoughts go way back to Genesis, the flood, and Noah's big adventure. Their hearts are on fire, wrapped in thorns, but glowing with a sacred light. Each sentence they speak has a life of its own. Treasures of wisdom and understanding, Alpha and Omega, the earth forming from a void. A police car pulled up to the curb. "Hey Jeremiah, out for a walk?" "I'm practicing the art of blessing," I told him, and he said, "Yeah, I can feel it."

Despite What They Say

I broke up with Salma in the summer of 2004 while I was working at the Army Navy Store in Dayton, Ohio. When I told her I wanted to date someone else, she punched me so hard my glasses flew across the room and hit the wall. I can't see a thing without them, so I felt around on the floor like a blind man—by the time I found my corrective lenses she was gone. I thought maybe she had cast a spell and what followed was seven years of bad luck. My signature Tarot card was The Hanged Man and the *I Ching* advised me, "Do not marry the maiden." One good thing happened during those seven years: I gave up smoking. Except for one or two gaspers every now and then. In 2012 I went down to Mexico and did a sweat ceremony with a Mayan shaman. He told me that the Mayan calendar is circular—there is no end of the world, even though the American news media had been forecasting the end for years. Despite what they say, creation keeps on going, one little bang after another. Trees fall, are reborn as houses and tables. Once the mojo gets going, it's hard to stop. After two hours in the sweat lodge I imagined a white jaguar was sitting across from me. Just last Sunday, at church, a woman in the first pew turned and looked me in the eye. When I see a tree I step outside myself.

Fender Bender

I was driving home and a woman ran into me. She pulled out of a side street and—*wham*—her car smacked into mine. The front of her car was badly damaged, but there wasn't a scratch on my new pickup. The cop who arrived a few minutes later was skeptical. "Are you sure your car hit his?" he asked the woman. She nodded, like this sort of thing happens all the time. "It's just not my day," she said. The cop bent down and looked at the side of my truck with a magnifying glass. "There's no evidence of damage," he said to me. "I know," I said. "Isn't that amazing. It's like I'm blessed in some special way." "So there was no accident and I can't report one," the officer said. "But what about *my* car," the woman said. "Look at those dents." One headlight was hanging from its socket. "Sorry," the cop said and got on his motorcycle and rode away. I turned to the woman. "Let's have a drink," I suggested. We walked to a pub, drank two bourbons straight-up, then wrapped our arms around the bartender and held him over our heads like muscle men. Two customers we thought were dead got up from their stools and did the hokey pokey. Police officers everywhere pressed their ears to the ground. An alarm went off in the *Bon Vivant*.

Plato's Classroom

All morning I've been waiting for an idea, something I can build on, like Plotinus sitting at his desk smelling the sea through a window into paradise. Am I too focused on "free will"? I wonder. I think of Saint Augustine, who did not look kindly upon the heretics in Rome. The sheep had been fleeced one too many times, he believed. His contemporary, John of Thebes, had been unable to distinguish himself from the brethren: *This is myself and this is myself,* he told Augustine when asked for some confirmation of *The Pandemonium Diaries*. Augustine answered with a riddle: *Why does time, during prayer, seem fractured or distorted?* Now I realize that the far future will be exactly the same as the distant past, and that Plato's vision of the future was actually a vision of heaven. He is living all eternity teaching philosophy to attentive students. Not just the ancient thinkers, but also Hegel, Heidegger, and even Derrida. Eventually, after what, in human terms, seem like millennia, Jesus opens the classroom door and leads the eager students outside on a sunny day. Is Plato alone in his classroom? Of course not. A few Gnostics and Essenes have signed up for what is now an elective. Some seek philosophy in order to stop thinking in riddles. Others ride the celestial highways round and round and round.

Chez Bizet

I don't mind that classes have been canceled and all the professors are on strike. It's a beautiful day—too beautiful to stay indoors: Let's roast a pig or buy a corsage for our favorite North Dakotan. Just last week, after the spring festival, at which the youngest performers were thrown violently to the ground, my worst headache was transformed into a practical joke. The woman in room 203 was running up and down the stairs naked. I tried to type up my notes, but the best ideas were frozen. Things weren't adding up: she loved me, but I loved someone else. The next day, while passing through a subway turnstile I heard a violinist playing *La jolie fille de Perth*. When I walked past the opera house, the composer's evil grandchildren were watching me with searchlight eyes. I miss those halcyon days on the Champs-Élysées, the summer I stood on my head at the Place de la Concorde and then drove quickly through Serbia and Montenegro, where I saw rainbows diving into the sea. Winter was no longer psychotropic. My friends were cool and weary, oh so weary, of the deadly sang-froid. I would have preferred something more upbeat, a day with sinners or the ancient corset of animal magnetism. In a minute, everything evaporated and I was alone on the shore with an armful of darkness.

III. A Light Went on in the Invisible Tower

I Should Never Have Hunched Over While Drinking a Tecate

My brother LaMarcus suggested I could "go all night" with just one bottle of Guinness and a can of Red Bull, but I tend to ignore his advice, so I wasn't sure if "going all night" was something that was good for the heart and soul and would help me on my journey forward. It was like I was looking through the wrong end of a telescope and all my plans were, you know, miniscule. I was five-three and suffered from "health problems," which my dad thought was some kind of code name for STDs. I asked my mother what she thought, but it was time for *The Price is Right* or *Breaking Bad*, I forget which, and she had zero interest in what might be happening in "real life." And now I'm distracted by the new *Ben-Hur*. Jack Huston is not Charlton Heston, but he has a closer walk with Jesus. "Hey, this is awesome," Dad says, getting excited as the chariot race shifts into high gear.

Waiting in Line

They are standing outside a theater, the handsome couple. He is wearing a blue scarf and tweed coat, she a short black jacket. He rode to the theater in a cab, a yellow cab with a sign on the roof: *Sabor Salem*. His apartment had been robbed, one of his car windows broken. He wants to tell the woman how he feels, but he senses that she is thinking of someone else. A young woman approaches, her face flushed. The train was crowded, a man on the train was rude. This is New York, she thinks, I've always been afraid of New York. Two men are standing next to her, waiting in line. One is unwashed, hairy, ill-kempt. The other well-dressed, business suit, gold watch, cigarbox smile. They share a smoke and talk about rattlesnakes, King Kong, wolves in sheep's clothing, a fire in a paper mill, the muscle car that ran out of gas. "The Pope is coming tomorrow," the hairy man says. "He has no place to stay." They laugh and slap each other on the back. A door opens in the building behind them. A woman and two Chihuahuas rush onto the sidewalk. A car stops. Horns blare. A huge black dog on the other side of the street opens its mouth like a cavern.

What They Don't Know About Your Country

Carson answers the phone. A sexy voice. "Would you like to have some fun? "Yes, I would," Carson says. "Do you know where the nearest Baptist church is?" She hangs up. He feels the heat rising through the floor, tickling his toes. The phone beeps again. His wife calling from up north. She's crying. What's wrong? "The back door blew open last night and the kitchen is full of snow. I'm sick and I don't feel like shoveling." He drops his towel on a chair, adjusts the air conditioning, looks out the window. People are running on the beach and playing volleyball. Some are dancing. "Well, I could hop on a plane and I'd be there in seven hours," he says. "By then the snow will have melted," she says. "I'll be OK. When are you coming back?" "Not for another month." "What's it like there?" "Warm and sunny. People are friendly. I try to tell them about winter, but they don't understand." "Neither do I," she says, and hangs up. He imagines a big snowdrift in their kitchen, bigger than the refrigerator, and the wood-burning stove heating the room and melting the snow—like a river in his imagination, washing away dishes, pots and pans, frozen food, their relationship, everything floating downstream into a boiling ocean.

Do Androids Dream of Real People?

It's early morning. I'm sitting in my car in a traffic jam thinking about the future. I just graduated from college and I'm working for a small book publisher, writing in my spare time. Do I want to write about "real life," I wonder, or make things up? Will I retreat into a world of imagination or venture forth, like an intrepid explorer, into the realm of forbidden knowledge? Can I act like a character in a novel or live a normal life as a writer of fabulous stories? Am I stuck in traffic or imagining myself sitting in a lunch room where people are laughing and telling jokes I don't understand? Fantasy and reality seem to intersect. Perceptions are altered. I have just started reading *Do Androids Dream of Electric Sheep?* and Rick Deckard has discovered that Rachael Rosen is an android. It reminds me of when I'm at work wondering which people are real and which are robots. "Most of us are operating from a hypnotically-induced sense of self," Isaiah, one of my co-workers, tells me at lunch. "We think who we seem to be is who we really are, but it's actually a false identity imposed on us as children or college students." While he is talking, I recall standing in the kitchen where I live in San Francisco watching eggs frying in a pan and wondering why I had been thinking negative thoughts about large corporations. Maybe I read too much. Or think too much about the books I read. Traffic is starting to move.

Hotel Minnesota

My neighbor went outside this morning and tried to measure the snowfall on his picnic table—his yardstick disappeared. I drove up to Bull Hill and found the superintendent of highways plowing the county roads. He had been plowing all night. Last Saturday, he and I were drinking at a pub and listening to the Eagles sing "Hotel California." When I lived in Placerville we were proud to be "above the fog and below the snow." But then my wife left, so I quit my job and moved to Minnesota. Yesterday, when I was fishing at Birch Lake, a largemouth bass jumped into my boat. The boat tipped over and I swam to shore. It snowed all night. My car wouldn't start. My neighbor lost his yardstick in a snowdrift. I do not think about Vietnam, the battles in the jungle, napalm, and helicopters flying overhead like wasps. Instead, I imagine the future, heavenly vistas, fields of wildflowers on the slopes of the Alps, my first face-to-face encounter with the Lord of the Realm. I will sit on a beach and watch the sun breaking over Pompei. I will sing songs and recite poetry with troubadours in Provence and ride a tunnel wave off the coast of Peru. I will remember the deep snow on the picnic table and the clouds in the fish's eye.

Mr. Wong

Joan was trying to remember a song she heard on the radio, something about a mom and dad dancing a waltz to a rock-and-roll song. "You can't waltz to rock," Joan said. Phil looked up from his bacon and eggs. The kitchen seemed to be moving slightly to the west. Could be the whole house, he reasoned. The wind outside was howling. The wind inside was a subtle harmony. Streets turned peacefully in circles around the village where they lived. At night he could see his neighbors through their windows glowing green and waving at each other. When the sun sank in the west, freedom was a shout from the heavens. Children ran here and there, climbing the far hills of eternity. "Our neighbors are wholesome, church-going hypocrites," he said to his wife. "There you go again," Joan said. "The church is different now—it's not like it was back in the '60s, when we were kids. They welcome nonbelievers, preach light petting, rather than abstinence. Many work in public relations, level-headed as they are, prime candidates for feel-good parties. Some are exotic dancers at the Elks Club. Mr. Wong is especially well-hung." Phil looked up from his laptop. "How do you know?" he asked.

Don't Get Me Wrong

My mother died on the day Shakespeare was born. I mean, on his birthday this year, not 400 years ago—she wasn't that old. She was quite young and the day of her death came unexpectedly, like the scene in the play when Hamlet stabs Polonius rather than his mother. This was disappointing for me in two ways. First, because my mother died in Arizona and like the song says, "There is no Arizona." And second, because Polonius was my best friend in high school and even though I haven't seen him in years, I had hoped to see him again at our tenth reunion. So maybe I won't go to the reunion—I'll stay home and read Shakespeare and watch Vikings slice and dice Anglos and Saxons on the History Channel. Why not? In the house across the street the Ferlinghettis are unholstering their negative emotions. In fact, our whole town is down the road a piece. We were brought up on turnip greens and bacon grease. Don't get me wrong—my mother was not a bad cook. She liked to sing in the shower. At her feet, our family was a graceful curve, a line connecting the dots in everyone's special story. We understood French philosophy and the theory of self. We marked time by whispering to one another. And when she died, we burned her body and let the river take the ashes.

Any Place on Earth Will Do

After a long trip I want to stretch out, feel my dog's tongue on my toes, lock down the gloom room, and get all frisky with neighbor Sue. And then the phone chirps and my best friend Atley has been arrested in Amsterdam. Or so the voice on the phone says, but I'm not really sure it's my best friend—it could be my uncle in Des Moines. Voices sound the same over long distances and each caldera is just a jumping-off point, a portal into the brain of a woman named Tulsa. She and I and Atley grew up in the same city and rode motorcycles together during the last days of the Cold War. He traveled west and she east. I stayed home and enrolled in Bible school—after each class, a light went on in the invisible tower. In my way of thinking, we are all breathing deeply in a vivid sort of duality. The unity of being, or something like it. Philosophy in 25 words or less. Heidegger cocksure of himself. To be honest, I am tired of living in Oklahoma where shoes are too tight. I want to be hip, grow vegetables in a state of unpredictability. Live hungry, let the lost children stampede themselves. But something is missing—a humming as loud as the breath of sound. When I fall asleep, life will start again, ideas without wings will wither in the alchemy of silence.

Golden Opportunities

I met Alyssa in Chicago, at a Michael Jackson concert. After the concert we went to a party and sat on the floor and talked about science fiction, Borges, robots on Mars, and *Forbidden Planet*. It was like we were the only two people in the room. When the party ended, we said good-bye and I didn't see her again. A few years later, at a Mariah Carey concert in San Francisco, I met a woman who looked just like Alyssa. Same jet-black hair and chocolate-brown eyes. After the concert, we sat on a bench in Golden Gate Park and talked about Jane Austen, *Journey to the Center of the Earth*, sacrifices to volcano gods, and Blackfoot trickster myths. When the night ended, she suggested we meet again, but I left the city a few days later. Chicago, San Francisco, cities in my rearview mirror. Atlantis, Middle Earth, Easter Island, the open road. As I think about it now, I wonder if all that moving around caused me to miss some golden opportunities. When I was in high school, one of my writing teachers suggested I reign in my imagination and try writing stories that were more true-to-life, like something you might find in *Reader's Digest*: "Hometown Heroes" or "13 Things Your Mother-in-Law Won't Tell You." I think she was right—there's a limited market for alien hijackings and Budweiser babes on the moon. But in the end, when we add it all up, will words really matter? Or will it be that moment when the hand of Zeus reaches down to pick you up and carry you off to Mount Olympus?

War Heroes

Grandpa didn't like to talk about the war. "I made fifty dollars a month," he said. "Fifty-two dollars when I was promoted to private first class." Grandma made seventy-five dollars a month. She was a lieutenant in the nurses' corps. She helped patch up guys when they were flown back from the front. "Your Grandpa was a hero," Grandma said. "He took out machine-gun nests with hand grenades and carried wounded soldiers to safety. He's just modest. At the battle of Bastogne he was shot through the lung and almost died. While he was lying in a trench bleeding, he had a vision of time beyond time, the creation of the world when the thunder gods brought life to our planet. When he woke up in the hospital, he understood that all the men on the battlefield were real people and not ghosts wearing uniforms." She waved her hand, powdered sugar drifted like snow across the kitchen counter. "When your grandfather was a boy he used bottle caps and train tickets for toy soldiers. There were no computer games or TV. We listened to *The Lone Ranger* on the radio." She cut another slice of huckleberry pie. "But we ate well. And we had electricity." She smiled at Grandpa. There was a strange light in his eyes, like he was seeing everything for the first time.

Mother's Day

We were driving from Dallas to Fort Worth and I fell asleep, but it didn't matter, because the highway is straight and, like my wheels, perfectly aligned. Dad was sitting beside me—he fell asleep, too, then woke up as we reached the city limits. "Where the hell are we?" he said and punched me in the arm. The car swerved, left the highway, and hit a billboard: IF YOU ARE CAUGHT SELLING ILLEGAL DRUGS YOU WILL SPEND THE NEXT 10 YEARS IN PRISON AND YOUR MOTHER WILL SPEND THE NEXT 10 YEARS WORRYING ABOUT YOU EVERY SINGLE NIGHT. I backed the car out of the ditch and drove the rest of the way to Abilene, Dad snoozing in the front seat. I dropped him at a bar and drove to my mom's house—she was lying in bed breathing through a respirator. There was so much oxygen in the room my head felt like a balloon. Her friend Al was sitting outside on the deck smoking a cigarette. I wished them Happy Mother's Day, then drove back to the bar and found Dad slumped in a booth, drinking a draft beer. I just sat there while he hated me. On a napkin I wrote: *Afraid of the sky, you cover your face with leaves of silk, clouds of dark blossoms rising and falling, as the wind carries each of you away.*

Desert Adventure

The last time I saw Bentley was at the Semiramis Hotel in Cairo. We had been up river to Abu Simbel, traded some gold for a night with Sheik Mahmoud's daughter, or so Bentley told me. I was so stoned on ganja I couldn't tell one oasis from another. In fact, Bentley, the sheik, and his alleged daughter-for-rent all sort of blurred together as we marched from Luxor to Memnon, two soldiers with hankies for helmets. "Maybe we should hike at night," Bentley suggested, "when it's cooler." Not a bad idea, I thought, then I envisioned the sheik's henchmen pursuing us on rabid camels. I reached into my rucksack and fondled my rawhide quirt and bullwhip. "I'll be ready when they come," I told Bentley, and he grinned like a homicidal maniac. Just then, two swimsuit-competition winners drove up in a Land Rover and offered us a ride. They had a cooler full of Bud and Bentley and I sat in the back seat and read the latest issue of *Sports Illustrated*. Next thing I knew I was at the airport and Bentley was a distant memory. Could any of this be true? Or was it all a dream? I looked up and saw an Air France 747 circling overhead. The Egyptian sky was a dusty mirror of black clouds and broken glass.

High School Confidential

Jason Storm was the new kid in school and we all imagined he was hipper than we were. He dressed like a model, had a killer smile and perfect teeth. Later we found out he shoplifted cigarettes from the 7-Eleven and strangled stray cats and hung their carcasses on telephone poles. From then on, we were suspicious of new kids and kept them at a distance. That worked pretty well until Melody Broadleaf arrived at school. Melody's hair was honey-blond and her eyes crystal-blue. Her smile could have melted an iceberg. Still, we were cautious. We didn't invite her to our weekend parties or hang out with her in the cafeteria. Jason Storm had been in jail for only a few months and the memory of those unfortunate stray cats was fresh in our minds. As it turned out, Melody was a model citizen. She sang in a church choir and collected toys at Christmas for underprivileged children. And then, after graduation, she was gone. She was awarded a scholarship at a college in another state and we never saw her again. Jason Storm served his time in the state penitentiary and we see him every five years at class reunions, even though, so far as I know, he failed to graduate from high school. He drives fast cars and wears fur coats. He's still the same.

Jungle Juice

A gorilla rang my doorbell. "Do you have any jungle juice?" he asked. "Just a small bottle of cranberry and vodka," I told him. "Will that do?" "Let's try it," he said. We sat on the couch and drank quietly for a few minutes, then he told me about his trip to Abu Simbel before the monument was lifted to a new location 65 meters above the Nile, how he traveled back in time and encountered Jesus at the Mount of Olives, and when his brother Cornelius threw a rock in the Cheyenne River and created a wave that inundated a village five miles downstream. "Being in that other world—the world of the imagination—is like finding a live bird on the moon," he said, "or appreciating fully the magic of life without television—nothing is exactly as it seems." He paused and looked at his empty glass. "This is good," he said, "Do you have more?" "I can mix another batch," I said. He drank a pitcherful, belched, stood up and scratched himself. "Time for bed," he said. "Where is your guest room?" I showed him. The next morning he awoke early and left for his job at Walmart. Why am I dissatisfied? I wondered as I watched him lumber down the street.

Voice of the Wilderness

"Let's not worry about the past or go downtown after sunset," Pa said. And Ma hit him with a frying pan. Later, when a wolf molested my grandmother, it seemed like something somewhere got mixed up: the ice on the mountains or the raving blue dawn. Everyday life is like a road paved through the ocean, a saint living in the refrigerator, or the slow arc of the thurible as the priest walks through the sanctuary. Does it matter if the sunlight is faded? So many houses are poorer because of the rain. I call my sister and a strange voice comes on the line—it sounds like someone reading a news report describing troop movements in Eastern Europe. My sister is talking to a man with a deep voice like a TV or radio commentator. "The truth is within us, not in some fantasy about politics and current events," the man says. And my sister says, "When spring arrives, what can we say about the snow?" "The eyes of the rivers wait for darkness," I whisper into the mouthpiece, but I don't think they hear me. I clear the dishes from the table and feed the dog. He looks at me like the dumb animal he is.

When the Sky Turns Red, We Will Sleep at the Buddha's Feet

A man with long blond hair is laughing. I see my reflection in his dark sunglasses. I am not laughing. I look sad, lonely, lost, afraid. When I close my eyes, I am wandering through a universe of star clusters, listening to the music of the spheres. Planets are like billiard balls in a solar system that reaches beyond infinity into another world where sorrow is unknown. I pinch my cheeks, splash water in my face. When I open my eyes, we are sitting in a garden beside a lake. "Would you like to learn something about the nature of human experience?" the blonde man asks, crossing his legs. "As long as I can keep my pen and a few sheets of paper," I answer. He smiles like he just thought of something funny. "A man owes me a thousand dollars," he says. "How can I get it back?" "When a shadow falls, don't pick it up," I advise him, although I am not sure this is the right answer. Clouds pass over the lake. A large raindrop descends slowly from the sky.

Richie Rich at Glacier Point

Tanya was wearing her Amélie-style, gnome-infested pajamas and I was sucking her toes in the back seat of her Mini Minor. We had been together about three weeks, dropping shoes, socks, and torrents of laughter along the highway. "Close your eyes and pretend you are Richie Rich," she said after we shoplifted a camera and two belts of five-hour energy boosters. No sir, we are not dumb-ass middle Americans in search of the golden toilet bowl. We are comrades in the Steampunk revolution, fish-eyed men wearing silky top hats, busty women strapped in leather corsets. Brains like paperweights, flaming tongues and bushes, pillars of fire. Everything just outside the borders of what I think of as my comprehension. Or happiness. I don't know what it is. But it's something, it must be. What we wonder most is how it will end—in some other reality, or pseudo-reality, along with the Mini Minor's frail children. We are not animals, but plants that can't stop moving. Last night we slept at Glacier Point and dreamed we were bears, sleek and white as snowdrifts.

My Life as a Horse

In a previous life, I was a horse. I was obedient and under-
stood the needs of men and women. I rarely stepped out
of line. Occasionally, I was aerophagous. But not when
people were nearby. I was sensitive. Just the mention of
horsehide made me shiver and I did not feel comfortable
at high noon. I remembered Gary Cooper, his ordeal in the
film. And then my veterinarian reminded me that Grace
Kelly saved Coop's life at the end of the movie and I felt
better. I stamped my hoof, just to feel my iron shoe hit the
ground. But this was not a sign of impatience. I was a
patient horse. I just loved to snort air. Air made me giddy
like I could gallop all day or leap a dozen barrels lined up
side by side. And even though I was swift, I did not show
off. I ran with a generous heart. I trotted like an elk on the
make. I galloped like an elephant with iron feet. And after
I died, I was reborn as a golden bee on a purple flower. I
was mayor of a small village, a monk in France, a river
flowing between stars. My wife saved my life.

Song of the Parking Lot

When Sylvia Plath was growing up in Winthrop, Massachusetts, she hoped she would some day live a contented life in London, go boating on the Thames, and ride in carriages through Hyde Park. Instead, she married Ted Hughes and they spent many unhappy years together. In 1960, after her first book of poems, *The Colossus*, was published, she went to New York to do a series of readings. One afternoon, in a grocery store in Queens, she noticed Walt Whitman squeezing an avocado. Sylvia said hello and invited him to her reading at Smith College. Walt said he was planning to drive across America and he wondered if she would like to join him. "Summer grows old quickly," Sylvia said. "That's true," Walt said, "but poems live forever. I am the open road, the oceans and mountains, the rivers and streams. Through me, the trees speak." Sylvia shook her head. "We cannot breathe the living water or drink the smoking stone." Walt nodded. "I guess you're right," he said and went outside and stood in the parking lot for a long time, trying to remember where he left his car.

Raindrops

Jack and Diane were lovers in high school. Soon after graduation, Diane discovered she was pregnant. Jack left in the fall for college. Diane named her baby Jacqueline. A few years later, Jack dropped out of college and moved to San Francisco where he sold drugs to street-corners addicts. After a few serious run-ins with the law, he got a job at a methadone clinic in the Mission District. Twenty years passed and Diane called to tell him his mother had died. He went back to Omaha for the funeral. He and Diane became lovers again and she moved to San Francisco to live with him. In Omaha, their daughter Jacqueline gave birth and named her new baby Joy.

After graduating from college, Joy moved to Brooklyn. She and Enrique live in the same apartment building on Clinton Street. They eat at the same restaurants, read the same romantic novels, walk the same streets on rainy nights, but they never meet, even though they believe that some day they will meet—eventually everyone finds the right person. Enrique hangs out at rooftop bars in Manhattan, but most of the women he knows seem vain and superficial. Joy hooks up now and then with people she meets at work or at the public library, but still feels alone. She is preoccupied with a frenzied spirit, the flesh of confiscated books, the mystery of too many raindrops.

Transfiguration

I had been in the city less than twenty minutes and my car was stolen. I called my mom and told her what had happened. "It's only money," she said. "We have insurance." On the train going home, the woman beside me was reading a book about Christian Science. On one page was a full-color reproduction of Bellini's painting of the Transfiguration. Peter, James, and John on their knees as God the Father speaks from a cloud: *This is my beloved son in whom I am well pleased.* The woman and I started talking about the Bible and I told her that my car had been stolen and my dad died a year ago and I've been unable to feel any joy in life. "Spiritual emancipation yields uncertain results," she said. "It's like a lantern submerged in a dark pool. Vision is impaired temporarily, then everything seems brighter and tastier—like lemons and chocolate. Forget the dream of dying for a moment and live in the consciousness of true being. Imagine—or visualize—a white rose in a blue vase: a soul adrift in an ocean of love. Eternal life belongs to those who live in the present. Be entirely in the moment and listen for the voice of truth. On the mountain of spiritual understanding, the Holy Spirit is speaking—death and stolen property have no dominion."

In the Beginning

It all started with a big bang, or *the* Big Bang. Out of chaos,
or The Void, came teenagers, truck drivers, and sissies.
Life followed. Plants, animals, and whatever I can see in
my rearview mirror. The wilderness, the Tampa Bay Buc-
caneers, Jean Lafitte, some lesser-known pirates, the Pitts-
burg Pirates, Charlton Heston, Hester Street, Avenue C,
uptown, downtown, the Riviera on Sundays after the
stores are closed. Today is beautiful, wonderful, enchant-
ed. Cells tremble with excitement. The horizon is tilted
like a ship at sea. I am a tree holding an armful of robins.
I am hiking in the Blue Ridge Mountains thinking about
The Last of the Mohicans and Magua plunging his knife into
Cora's breast and Hawkeye falling to his knees and the
eyes of warriors everywhere filling with tears. It was a
beginning of sorts. Time united to its divine principle.
Imagination set free.

Rock Me, Babe

At the top of the stairs, the Queen of Hearts puts her hands on my shoulders and kisses me hungrily on the lips. I fall down the stairs, like Alice down the rabbit hole. When I wake up, it's 1967, the Summer of Love. I'm driving down California Street and the Doors are singing "Touch me, babe." Dr. Gonzo is in the bathtub, about to peak on acid. Three weeks later, we are trying to squeeze twenty years of boredom into a single night of debauchery. On Haight Street, I see a sign that makes no sense. "The revolution has already happened," it says, "and you missed it."

Notes:

In "East Window," the quotation is from Virgil: "Round the wide world in banishment we roam, Forced from our pleasing fields and native home." (*Eclogues*, Book I, line 3, as translated by John Dryden).

**Poems in this book previously appeared
in the following publications:**

Poetry East: "The Art of Blessing," "Plato's Classroom"
Tampa Review: "Despite What They Say"
Washington Square Review: "Fender Bender"
elsewhere: "Waiting in Line"

About the Author

Michael Malan was born in Missoula, Montana, and grew up "on the road." Most of his early memories originated in the back seat of a car. He's done more road trips than Jack Kerouac.

He is grateful to the following teachers and professors who encouraged him to persevere over the years: Mary Baxter Foley, Heather Strachan Foley, Dennis Schmitz, A.R. Ammons, Robert Morgan, and Peter Sears.

In 1999, Malan and Sears founded a small press, Cloudbank Books, in Corvallis, Oregon. Their first book was *Millennial Spring: Eight New Oregon Poets. Cloudbank*, a literary journal (cloudbankbooks.com), was launched in 2009. Malan currently serves as editor.

He is the author of *Overland Park* (Blue Light Press, 2017), a collection of poetry and flash fiction. His work has appeared in *Epoch, Cincinnati Review, Tampa Review, Washington Square, Grist, Denver Quarterly, Poetry East, Hayden's Ferry Review, Potomac Review,* and many other journals.

www.ingramcontent.com/pod-product-compliance
Lightning Source LLC
Chambersburg PA
CBHW032024090426
42741CB00006B/724